SPECTRUM OF LOVE

Happiness always
Love
Miles

SPECTRUM of LOVE

Walter Rinder

Celestial Arts Publishing
Millbrae, California 94030

First Printing, January 1973
Second Printing, February 1973
Third Printing, September 1974

Library of Congress Card No.: 72-96369
ISBN 0-912310-19-7 Paper Edition
ISBN 0-912310-20-0 Cloth Edition
Made in the United States of America

"I love you."

There is a much greater

motivation than simply

my spoken words.

For me to love is to commit myself,

freely and without reservation.

I am sincerely

interested in your happiness

and well being.

Whatever your needs are,

I will try

to fulfill them and will bend

in my values depending on the

importance of your need.

If you are lonely and need me,

I will be there.

If in that loneliness you need

to talk, I will listen.

If you need to listen,

I will talk.

If you need the strength of

human touch, I will touch you.

If you need to be held,

I will hold you. I will lie naked

in body with you if that be

your need. If you need fulfillment

of the flesh,

I will give you that also,

but only through my love.

I will try

to be constant with you so that you

will understand the core of my

personality and from that

understanding you can gain

strength and security that

I am acting as me.

I may falter with my moods.

I may project, at times, a strangeness

that is alien to you, which may

bewilder or frighten you.

There will be times

when you question my motives.

But because people are

never constant and are as

changeable as the seasons,

I will try to build up within you

a faith in my fundamental attitude

and show you that my inconsistency

is only for the moment and

not a lasting part of me.

I will show you love now.

Each and every day,

for each day is a lifetime.

Every day we live,

we learn more how to love.

I will not defer

my love nor neglect it,

for if I wait until tomorrow,

tomorrow never comes.

It is like a cloud in the sky,

passing by.

They always do, you know!

If I give you kindness

and understanding,

then I will receive your faith.

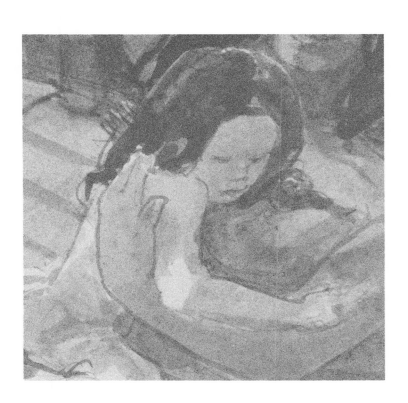

If I give hate and dishonesty,

I will receive your distrust.

If I give you fear and am

afraid, you will become afraid

and fear me.

I will give to you what I need

to receive.

To what degree (amount) I give love

is determined by my own capability.

My capability is determined by the

environment of my past existence

and my understanding of

love,

truth,

and God.

My understanding is determined

by my parents, friends,

places I have lived and been. All

experiences that have been fed into

my mind from living.

I will give you as much

love as I can.

If you will show me how to give more,

then I will give more.

I can only give you as much as you

need to receive or allow me

to give.

If you receive all I can give,

then my love is endless and

fulfilled.

If

you receive a portion (part)

of my love,

then I will give others

the balance I am capable of giving.

I must give all that I have,

being what I am.

Love is universal.

Love is the movement of life.

I have loved a boy, a girl,

my parents, art, nature, children and

myself — only to the depth that

I know myself.

All feelings in life I find

beautiful.

No human being or

society

has the right to condemn

any kind of love

I feel

or my way of expressing

         it, if I am sincere,

sincerity being the honest realization

of myself,

and there is no

hurt

or pain

intentionally involved in my life

or any life my life

touches.

I want to become a truly loving spirit.

Let my words, if I must speak, become

a restoration of your soul.

But when speech is silent,

does a man project the great

depth of his sensitivity.

When I touch you,

      or kiss you,

            or hold you,

        I am saying

a thousand words.